Genius Floored:
Alphabet of Days

SOARING PENGUIN PRESS
LONDON UK

Genius Floored:
Alphabet of Days

Edited by Ruth O'Callaghan

Genius Floored: Alphabet of Days
edited by Ruth O'Callaghan

Published by
Soaring Penguin Press
4 Florence Terrace
Kingston Vale
London
SW15 3RU
www.soaringpenguinpress.com

First Edition: July 2012

10 9 8 7 6 5 4 3 2 1

This edition copyright © 2012
Poems included are copyright © their respective creators

ISBN: 978-1-908030-05-4

No part of this publication may be reproduced (except as brief extracts in reviews) without permission of the publisher, nor be circulated in any form of binding or cover other than that in which it is published.

Printed in the UK

With thanks to Christine Johnson, Lynn Foote and Adele Ward for their constant and unselfish help in staffing the venues.

Acknowledgements

Rosie Bailey's poem *Here and Now* was published in Marking Time (Peterloo).

Connie Bensley's *Perspectives* published in Central Reservations (Bloodaxe).

Mimi Khavati's poem *The Swarm* was first published in *Poetry Review*

Ruth O'Callaghan's poem *While Waiting for Bad News* was published in *A Lope of Time* (Shoestring 2009)

Anne Stevenson's poem *Not a Hook* was first published in *Other Poetry*

Anne Stevenson's poem *In the Museum of Floating Bodies and Flammable Souls* was published in the *Times Literary Supplement* and in her *Collected Poems* (Bloodaxe 2006)

If any acknowledgement has been inadvertently omitted the editor apologises unreservedly.

Contents

Acknowledgements		6
Foreword		10
A letter from Geoffrey Roper (Revd) Lumen Church Secretary		12
Before the Crib	John F. Deane	14
While Waiting For Bad News	Ruth O'Callaghan	16
Hedge Bird	Matthew Hollis	21
Orange Ribbon and Tiger Lilies	J. S. Watts	22
Snow	Malcolm Wroe	23
The Swarm	Mimi Khalvati	24
Honeycomb	Alison Brackenbury	25
War Graves	Gillian Henchley	26
Angle of View	Anna Avebury	27
Haytiming	Ann Pilling	28
Landings of the Deceased	Donald McDonnell	29
5 Minutes in the Life of Paris & Helen	William Oxley	30
Portents	Jill Townsend	32
The Owl Man	Annemarie Cooper	33
St Pachomius	Lyn White	34
In the Museum of Floating Bodies and Flammable Souls	Anne Stevenson	36
Ammonite	Louise Warren	37
My Ancestress	Lauri Kubuitsile	38
We Are Legend…We Are Myth	Donall Dempsey	39
Moss	Tania Hershman	40
Downside Lullaby	Anne Ballard	41

Perspectives	Connie Bensley	42
Not a Hook, not a Shelf, maybe a Song?		
	Anne Stevenson	43
Turning Point	Clare Booker	44
Salmon fighting upstream	Lynn Foote	45
Transmigration	Caroline Vero	46
Off Limits	Hugo Steer	47
A Moment of Shy	Jeremy Langrish	48
Sociology	Josh Ekroy	49
Vision	Christopher Morgan	50
The Girl in the Polka dot Dress		
	Peter Lavery	51
Tea Dance	Caroline Vero	52
The Harbour Bar, Toronto	Anne Ballard	53
Twilight song	Barry Jones	55
Here and Now	R V Bailey	56
Dad	Kaye Lee	57
Violin	Vicky Olliver	58
for Molly at 100	Kaye Lee	59
Snapshot	Maureen Duffy	60
Last Rites	Dorothy Phillips	61
Via Cola di Rienzo, Rome	Lyn White	62
Under London	Brian Ball	63
The Journey	Hannah Kelly	64
Amsterdam refocussed	Juliet Troy	65
Sign Your Name, Kafka	Tim Harris	66
Bergkamen Power Station	Dennis Tomlinson	67
Who's Looking?	Frances Thompson	68
Votive Offering	Alan Price	69

At Blake's Lock	*Claire Dyer*	70
Birling Gap to Bristol in an Old Red Citroen with the Sun-Roof Open		
	Chrissie Williams	72
They'll Never Tame Billy Caspar		
	David Osgerby	74
Black Dog	*Peter Lavery*	76
two black dogs	*Juli Jana*	77
Tomato	*Ann Barefoot*	78

Foreword

The Camden/Lumen Poetry Series has experienced another successful year with fine poems being read by such major poets as Anne Stevenson, who has also kindly donated two poems to this anthology. Additionally, the stars of the 2010 Aldeburgh Festival including Imtiaz Dharker, Matthew Caley and Innua Ellams, amongst others, and poetry from such diverse sources as Adnan Al-Sayegh, Ros Barber and Catherine Smith have stimulated the twice monthly audiences. Another highlight of the year was the reading by His Grace The Archbishop of Canterbury, Rowan Williams, a fine poet who generously included other poets in his reading.

The poets from the floor had the opportunity to read before these luminaries as well as before the publishers who also support the Cold Weather Shelter, Cinnamon Press and Shoestring to name but two. Particular mention must be made of Soaring Penguin Press the sponsor of this anthology and Ward Wood who sponsor the competition. Of course, grateful thanks should also be given to Carol Ann Duffy who generously continues to be our patron and has agreed once more to select the winner of the competition.

Other Camden/Lumen evenings have been given to magazines and groups such as the Highgate Poets and Ver Poets as well as to individuals including those who, summer and winter, come on the first Friday or third Tuesday of each month to support the project. To all these a huge thank you and to also all the contributors to this anthology including John F. Deane, Mimi Khalvati, Matthew Hollis, Connie Bensley and Maureen Duffy.

These evening could not take place without the loyal band of volunteers who give up long summer evenings in the garden and brave the bitter cold of winter to collect money on the door, serve wine or sell books and raffle tickets.

Any of you who have attended one of the evenings will recognise the names in the front of the book and will also possibly know the 'back-up' team – poets who volunteer if the usual team are unavailable. However, few will recognise the name Geoffrey Roper who leaves his warm home whenever necessary to lock up after a Lumen Poetry event. Geoffrey has kindly agreed to add a few words about Lumen the church.

Ruth O'Callaghan

A letter from Geoffrey Roper (Revd)
Lumen Church Secretary

Thank you for supporting the cold weather shelter by the purchase of this book.

Lumen United Reformed Church's building was constructed in three centuries. The under-floor basement ('crypt' if you want to be spooky) is brickwork of 1827 built to take a heavy twin-towered Scots church. The brick tower, walls and motorway-concrete arches are 1960s war damage replacement. The conical 'shaft of light' space to withdraw for prayer and meditation is part of the 21st-century rebuild along with the white, light, stone-floored space in which these poems have been read.

With the building's transformation the church took a new approach. We took the name 'Lumen' for the light that enlightens every one. We believe Jesus is the light of the world and we know that people come to the light in different ways, not all of which will fit exactly with what our kind of reformed protestant Christian churches believe and preach. But we want you to feel welcome. We are willing to take you seriously or just give you space to listen and speak, reflect and prepare to act.

However you choose to act following reflection we hope you find fruitful outcomes. We shall continue to be concerned for people around including those who find themselves without shelter in cold weather. Though we no longer host the night shelter in Lumen's building we are glad to associate with C4WS Homeless Project (Community of Camden Churches Cold Weather Shelter project; administered by CARIS Camden, registered charity 1121919) and to see the proceeds of this book and Poets' Evenings go to the project.

Lumen also cares about poor and underprivileged peoples in the wider world. Commitment for Life is our church's avenue to support, inform and campaign for justice for the world's poor. We seek achievement of the millennium development goals in troubled countries as much as peaceful ones.

Reflection and action are two sides of a whole life. If we only receive and reflect we leave no trace on our times; if our life is filled with activity leaving 'no time to stand and stare' we become hollow. Lumen is here to reflect the light we receive, as we believe, from the light of the world. You will always be welcome to our reflective worship services and music as well as the poetry evenings. And there's a nice Café attached, week-day-times.

Geoffrey Roper (Revd)
Lumen Church Secretary

Before the Crib

Unprecedented warmth had kept the herd
out in the fields till Advent; I saw their breathing, mornings,
hover over them like a cloud; later I heard

snuffling and jostling in the slatted shed, cumbersome
flesh confined, the occasional clang of iron like a deadened
bell ringing. Christmas, I knelt before the crib to see

the ox, watchful over the newly born who held, already,
both hands high in blessing; straw leaked from the patched roof,
Joseph stood, bland and painted, one hand broken off

at the elbow; I sniffed for the stench of cattle in cramped
spaces, finding it difficult to hold belief that here
is God's handiwork, here eternity has crawled into restricted

times and places, closing the distances between divinity
and dearth, between the heavens and the run-down church;
I wanted everything to change, I was a child, longing,

but without the words to plead. Now I pray, out
of the tragedy that is the history of our endeavour, to find
eternity in the bones of time, malice and greed subsumed

 in the outspread hands of the Christ, pray for faithfulness
beyond all guile, that we who are made of a yielding clay
may be, in deed, far more than we imagine.

John F. Deane 2011

While Waiting For Bad News

April is the cruellest month...
　　　T.S.Eliot

　　　　1

How can one letter weighing only a few grams
　　hold so much time suspended?

　　　What have they not told you?
　　　　What have I not?

　　　　***

You are my Seven Sisters
walked in snow and rain,
my winter sun hanging low
　　in a ragged sky.

Sweeter than the apple in the attic
stored till winter's end you are
the pasture where lions and lambs lie
the garden in which the wren rests.

Where will I run to, where hide
when winds rip trees from roots,
boats from moorings? Why, to you,
　　my anchor, my anchor.

2

Yet how did we start?
How could I have known love?

I had only the word for it
and tears did not come easily.

I was the poppy blazing red
your blaze of red, your stain
your runnel of blood

you were the pull of the moon
the shadow in the night
my darkness and my light

I was the day to your moon
the sun to your night
the burn of your day.

Yet water on stone
was not slower in its siege
than your constancy.

3

What eclipse let love steal across my sky?
    I did not see it.

What word was brushed from your lips to mine?
    I did not feel it.

What prayer was whispered in cathedral dark?
    I did not hear it.

But the smell of salt whipped on wind that tears
    your hair, your skin and the taste….
        God, the taste of you!

4

Were you a bird I'd eat the skin, bone, feathers of you.

Though I would save one bone, one feather,
not as a keepsake for that would be within me,
— having gorged your strength, your gentleness —
but to make a mark on clay or cuneiform, papyrus
or paper, use your bone to press keys, your iridescent
feather for a quill to form letters in the old way.

The alphabet of days is lodged in you
without you there is no holy Sunday
only Wednesday's child, full of woe.

Where will I take my sorrow?
The house cannot hold it
and the garden has its own rue.

S

Is there no prayer, no novena
to chant at Lourdes or Fatima,
no cockleshell in hat at Compostella?

If Easter comes early will Taxco
be empty, Seville's mountains
not thrum to resurrection drums?

What will I do now for my fool in April?
Why will you leave your fool in April?
    When the children chant
      Spring forward, Fall back
        What am I to do?

Ruth O'Callaghan

Hedge Bird

You're almost home. You've been numb
a long time. You didn't see the daylight slip out,
nor the fieldfares raiding the windfalls;
you didn't notice the holly in fruit,
or the wind lift wild garlic and whin
to your nose. Dusk gloves the hill;
soon the woods will back into shadow.
You could lose your way, even still.

Something is calling from the thicket.
You know the song, it was with you
when you started. Try not to think
you can find it with your eyes, reach out
and you'll only silence it. Listen.
The world comes in by the ear,
nudging the spirit to here and there,
waking the heart-step, conjuring the air.

Turn into the lane, the house is in view.
She loves you. You will make it through.

Matthew Hollis

Orange Ribbon and Tiger Lilies

I sang us to bed in a blaze
of orange ribbon and tiger lilies,
but have no voice for the passing
of our hour. Let others mourn,
I shall close up like a flower
sensing an absence of light.

I shall go back to the earth,
escaping the ravages of first frost.
I shut silently, leave singing to the birds.
There are no tiger lilies in winter
and our ribbons are already
mud splashed and ragged.

J. S. Watts

Snow

Surreptitiously it covers our sensibilities in the night.
Artefacts natural and man-made clothed in virgin white.

We awake to roofs, trees, roads purified;
wounds cauterised, camouflaged by light.

Phenomena both grotesque and beautiful, veiled out of sight.
We stand in it up to our ankles, filled with delight.

Malcolm Wroe

The Swarm

Snow was literally swarming round the streetlamp like gnats.
The closer they came, the larger they grew, snow-gnats, snow-bees,

and in my snood, smoking in the snow, I watched them.
Everyone else was behind the door, I could hear their noise

which made the snow, the swarm, more silent. More welcome.
I could have watched for hours and seen nothing more than specks

against the light interrupting light and away from it, flying blind
but carrying light, specks becoming atoms. They flew too fast

to become snow itself, flying in a random panic, looming close
but disappearing, like flakes on the tongue, at the point of recognition.

They died as they landed, riding on their own melting as poems do
and in the morning there was nothing to be seen of them.

Instead, a streak of lemon, lemon honey, rimmed the sky
but the cloud-lid never lifted, the weekend promised a blizzard.

I could have watched for hours and seen nothing more than I do now,
an image, metaphor, but not the blind imperative that drove them.

Mimi Khalvati

Honeycomb

It is too beautiful to eat.
Knife crumbles it from gold to dark.
Our keenest edge cannot stay sharp
while in our walls, which seemed so strong,
damp murmurs with the evening sleet.
I wonder if I live too long

but then I taste the honeycomb,
its waxen white upon my teeth,
its liquid sun which hides beneath.
Small deities, of wind or moon,
behold me. In my shabby room
I am a god. I lick the spoon.

Alison Brackenbury

War Graves

No one lives here now, none pass by.
They lie alone, three unknown sailors
set apart, graves facing seaward
out across the slow Atlantic swell,
their stones stark against a windblown sky,
a mark of no identity.
Each is placed in line as if in life
they might have been good friends.
Most likely all were in their teens.
Water tumbled flotsam.

Those bones will slide beneath the turf
and drift towards the headland's edge
that year by year erodes. Silt bound up
with heather roots and grass
that whistled in the western gale
will slip once more beneath the tide.

Gillian Henchley

Angle of View

I caught them, one, half-blind, head
tipped back, his eye hooking me
from beneath a blood-stained bandage,
crumpled packet of Pall Mall at his feet.

The other, curled like a tired child,
wounded head lodged
in the crook of his buddy's arm;
blood brothers snared in a shell-hole
in the palm-fringed mountain side.

Caught, the cry of the out-stretched
hand, nails bitten to the quick, held
for a second stretched to breaking,
life fraying to its end. A shutter-click
set the spool whirring, winding closer
to the final frame.

Anna Avebury

Haytiming

Through closed car windows all the way home
I smelt hay, its thin sweet fragrance.
They worked all yesterday

and some already lies in long green bricks
on bristly fields, the rest like swathes of hair
still waits for the machine.

I step across our threshold
Virtute non Verbis spelt in tiles
and think of old Julys

of men who walked out of this house
to the Somme, to Caen;
up this lane a boy brought telegrams.

I climb steadily, going west,
to a shaved meadow where the dog
careers about, tossing the loose hay.

Below, the quilted land thrums with mowing,
while a horse big enough to pull gun carriages
sleeps in the shade.

Ann Pilling

Landings of the Deceased

Last night it was on the news again
the same mundane item
The Landings of the Deceased
When will it ever cease?

A quintet this time, terribly sad
precious to their grieving loving tribes
and their traumatised comrades
as the fingers of our hands

A respectful, gentle, cortege gathers
Uniformed with Union Jacks and flowers
for the silent five within
and the subdued multitude without

They will be flanked and proudly greeted
by the tacit streets of Wooton Bassett
Undertakers parading in meticulous step
providing A Superior Funeral

The suave rationale of Number 10
will never, ever, resurrect them
as for the meaning, perhaps, one day
a Tacitus will draft the evidence

Donald McDonnell

5 Minutes in the Life of Paris & Helen

A hot dry day but as ever windy:
the sea-smell over the plain excitingly randy
but for that other smell hated by ladies
the cold grey stink of Hades.

Spartan women are a trifle coarse
have grace of face but throats that're hoarse:
Helen spat pips, swore, drank local nectar
and smiled at Paris but thought of Hector.

Paris of course was very beautiful
effetely game but no more dutiful
than she: their relationship never easy
unlike that of Hector and Andromache.

Last night the stars were bitter and they'd rowed,
Now at breakfast she looked cowed
but wasn't. To Paris she'd make amends:
he'd accept her and Hector were 'just friends'

and nothing more ('worse luck!' she thought).
Her life in Troy had really come to nought.
Smooth-talker Paris with his golden sentences
had got her there under false pretences!

And Sparta, which had also bored her
with its lack of fashion, its simple fare
and rage for outdoor activities,
now seemed a home compared to this

marble metropolis on the plain of death.
Helen flashed a sad glance from beneath
her pale pentelic brows –
why must love always lead to rows?

Beyond, on that greenly shimmering plain,
lay thousands of her kinsmen slain –
among them maybe Menelaus who used to fart in bed.
While here a scowling glamour boy scratched his head.

'Aphrodite, Aphrodite!' she sighed as tears came.
(Paris rose abruptly and left the room.)
As Helen wept a sense of tragedy, of unease
descended forever on the history of Greece.

William Oxley

Portents

The moon is looking down
into our goldfish bowl
but from straight overhead,
brighter than usual,
and we are not ourselves.

A few evenings ago
she screeched like a comet
through the sky as my train
swung one way, round a bend,
then the other: so strange

it was easy to see
how terror could arrive
from nowhere, dividing
us from one another,
from possibility.

Tonight she's more relaxed
and in a playful mood
might put a finger down
to stir the atmosphere,
see us dissolve as dreams.

Jill Townsend

The Owl Man

Who am I? said the Owl Man
when they found him on the sand
but none of them could answer,
this wasn't what they planned.

The sun –the sun –my enemy,
he clutched his aching head.
They tactfully removed his wings
and helped him into bed.

He lay inert, he scarcely breathed
until the moon was new
then wrote a careful note of thanks,
retrieved his wings and flew.

Annemarie Cooper

St Pachomius*

If ever I decide to cross the Amazon
or navigate the Rio de la Plata
I'll beg the protection of Pachomius.
I see him now,
crocodile stepping stones
lining up to bear him over the Nile.

I'll not wear shoes or boots
but feel tough scales
under my feet.
Maybe I'll stretch myself
the length of their backs
lean down into vast jaws
assess the sharpness
of each conical tooth
turn and lie under tropical skies
bask in the sun
ride on the rough, ridged skin.

Saints are less invoked these days -
relics of little interest, but I think
a metatarsal or the proximal phalanx
from Pachomius will serve me well
in hostile spaces. I'll carry it
strung round my neck on a leather lace -
stroke it in time with my prayers
as I dance lightly along a bridge
of closely packed reptilia.

"After this, so much trust had the blessed Pachome learned to place in God … the crocodiles, if ever he had necessarily to cross the river, would carry him with the utmost subservience, and set him down at whatever spot he indicated" (Dionysus)

Lyn White

In the Museum of Floating Bodies and Flammable Souls
For Angela Leighton

Painters who painted the flights of martyrs for money,
Who filled the drapery of saints with rose-tinted oil,
Had to please rich patrons with trapeze acts of the body,
Since no one can paint the electricity of the soul.

My lady in her blue silk cowl must by now be topsoil;
She swans into Heaven, almond eyes uplifted in piety.
My lord kneels at prayer in a cassock, blade at his heel;
Not a single cell of him sings of his wealth and charity.

While in Hell – well preserved in the water church of Torcello –
The wicked receive their deserts. Disembowelled or dismembered,
They are set upon eternally, yet their bodies alone are touched;
Unless souls flushed out of the flesh are the flames that torch them.

No wonder evil is interesting and goodness pitifully dull.
Torture of the body symbolises torture of the mind –
Though burning in the bonfires of conscience is hardly confined
To a hell for bad Italians – saved by being damned so well.

Anne Stevenson

Ammonite

He lays his spine against the slippery green,
the sea is out, his bones exposed
and a hospital gown rucked up
into a foam of dirty yellow around his knees.

Pale shapes appear on a dark screen.
He knows this is the stone of him split open.
Pain comes as an ache, as splinters,
he feels it as a hammer strike.

Later he curls up inside the dust of a room
built in layers of old books,
crumbling stacks of paper,
the marbling together of unwashed clothes.

The geological formations of his life
petrifying as he lies pressed in the contours
of his bed. Forgetting all else
but who will discover him.

Louise Warren

My Ancestress

They say she lived in a cave, dark, likely with bats.
Her mystical and me - practical as dirt
Yet finally something resonates inside
At the same wavelength on which she travelled
And I think of the one word
That never sat familiar on my tongue: Family.

I wonder did they chase her there? Somehow I doubt it.
A witchy woman is never chased. She chose her cave.
I see her hair, long and tangled. Maybe a cursory look
would uncover sticks brought from the southern reaches,
From where she came, to the icy north in search of freedom.
The opposite trip from mine, though exactly identical too.

I'm happy to know that somewhere a strand of feral,
feminine DNA, untainted and pure, hiding, in the powerhouse
of my body, belongs to her. Perhaps the essence of us both.

Her bits make me want to look behind to where I come from,
the place I fled. Where everything was unfamiliar and strange.
She has sent out a torch light, for me alone, I think,
Over generations and time, over distances.
And for the first moment, I am connected.

Lauri Kubuitsile

We Are Legend...We Are Myth

"DonallSeanie...SeanieDonall!"

My uncle & me
escaping from my auntie's voice

I sitting in the saddle
of his neck

his curls
my reins

my uncle hearing
voices in his head

afraid of others
who hunt his thoughts

wanting to keep
himself for himself

our beings fused
into one joyfulness

uncle & boy
morphing into centaur

we are legend
we are myth.

Donall Dempsey

Moss

The moss of his skin
began to grow
on the surface of mine

and then in bed
tiny daisy heads fell
on the pillow between us.

Tania Hershman

Downside Lullaby

Your head is growing heavy on my shoulder,
your slow breath tells me you will soon be snoring.
The duvet's on your side, it's getting colder
and even bliss eventually gets boring.

I know that you can lie like this till morning:
if shaken, you'll roll over on your back
and up the volume, like a hazard warning
for earthquake, smog or terrorist attack.

My right arm's gone to sleep, I'm getting cramp
in both my calves. I'm wired to every noise:
that tap's still dripping, and I'm sure it's mice
I hear behind the skirting board. I'm damp,
sweaty and sticky. As with all life's joys:
the greatest pleasures have the highest price.

Anne Ballard

Perspectives

When it comes to rewriting the past
we are all into faction:

last week's *faux pas* can be re-choreographed,
last month's extravagance taken in to fit

and last year's love affair totally edited -
the roles re-cast, the story line strengthened

and one's own part adapted and rendered
more rational. Darker areas of betrayal and folly

are lost, with clever lighting
and the use of perspective.

All it takes is time, rehearsal
and one's own gullibility.

Connie Bensley

Not a Hook, not a Shelf, maybe a Song?

'Love is too frail a hook to hang a life on.'
After the thrills of Ecstasy or booze,
The rites of hymen meet the wrongs of women,
And love begins to ease loose from its screws.

Becomes a shelf to raise a family on –
Love on a mortgage and a nine-to-five
Wearing away in blameless repetition,
The telly, Tesco's, kids, a four-wheel drive.

So where is love? Love is the under-chorus.
Everyone knows it, beats it, hums it, *Luv*
As it should have been and maybe sometimes was.
I hope it's love these shopping faces dream of,

Hungry Miss Pink Hair with her iPod ear;
Sad Mrs Pushchair, pregnant every year.

Anne Stevenson

Turning Point

White gabardine, cinched,
the wrong kind of heels;
she's discovering new muscles,
executes a three point turn,
shrieks on the paving shine,
(shameful wheels)
leaves behind the hellebores
and winter jasmine,
heads for the merest hint
of pansy sweetness,
indigo, scarlet, piebald whites,
leans further in for the perkiest pot;
his brooch - two salmon leaping -
less tight at her throat.

Clare Booker

Salmon fighting upstream

Go on then, hurl that tiny muscle
into the spume, tear out every sinew,
burn up all the phosphorus your body
stored in its surge through the deep-blue salt,
moodle in the shallows; up there the sky -
there are always going to be bears,
their long muzzles and shaggy fronds,
the lascivious care with which they lick
your bloody pulp out, standing inanimate
in the waterfall; through that gate
you get to the gravels and rubbing up
with your patched-up, shagged-out mate,
out of you tumble these perfect pink planets,
but it is that bullying battle you were born for.

Lynn Foote

Transmigration

The nomadic wildebeest has made a continent its own
pouring across open plains for a thousand miles
to feed, to drink, to breed, and in its wake
a realm of animals is sated, or else dies
whilst you have simply crossed these lowland hills
to take yourself away from me.
In autumn, leaves pungent beneath my feet
I pick rose hips, seek chestnuts to roast
on your open fire though you are vagrant miles away.
I eat my fill of you in hazelnuts and blackberries.

Caroline Vero

Off Limits

You'll never be my wife
tied to common life
but what I'd give to call you friend
two Pimms perhaps
across a cherished garden seat
where lovers often meet

I'd go for that
your wit and laughter fills the air
below the evening's scented sun
catching light in prettied hair
off limits to caress
will forever be my fate
but I would love you none the less.

Hugo Steer

A Moment of Shy

Two bound by decorum, each
vulnerable beyond their pride
as children released
from the habit of good behaviour.

Hip and bum in jean low slung
swaying in rhythm. Bodies
frames on which to hang clothes.
Frames alone and small patches of skin
or frames and brighter colour together.

Fragrances, warm, embracing
or sharp and tingling
to turn a nose, a head in savour,
wondering if contrived with natural odour
a harbinger of morning, evening smells.

Glimpses of each other in secret
from side, from behind.
seemingly dispossessed of themselves,
possessed of each other.
Here, tension in decorum, exhilarating,

sharing joy, sharing restraint, or nowhere to go.
Restrained to the appropriate,
wondering how to break free,
and what might happen if they do,
and what if they do not.

Jeremy Langrish

Sociology

Alone is allowed to be morose
Alone's debates are never resolved
Alone is social as trees are social
If Alone screams in a deserted spot it is not Alone
Speak for Alone as Alone can't speak for itself
Alone is the point
Alone is afraid of choking to death on a piece of gristle while eating stew
Alone the electric charge through the fruit in the bowl
Alone will rise again some day
Alone is all saintliness like a poodle
Alone sleeps in the niche under your tongue
Alone sees everything whole
Alone doesn't wish it hadn't said that
Alone is pleasantly sad but that counts for nothing
Alone is everything that counts for nothing
Alone is also a talking money plant
Alone is the yawn in the necessary conversation
Alone will marry you and stay married to you
You don't know Alone's agenda because Alone is being polite
Alone conforms only to Alone
Alone will sink its teeth into your shoulder for no reason
Alone trumpets its own blown phrases to itself
Alone has an astute ear for self-mockery
Alone is on the beach making dams in the streams
that flow from the spiky grass to the sea

Josh Ekroy

Vision

When I saw her,
        There in my street,
Unexpected,
        Supposed to be somewhere else,
I thought she was a beautiful apparition -
        I was seeing what I wanted to see.

And I turned,
        Turning the key,
And saw that it was her
A lovely reality.
        She smiled - we spoke - but still she went,

Like a vision,
        Not fading,
But going where
        I'd supposed her to be.

Christopher Morgan

The Girl in the Polka dot Dress

She said "Looking back
the best thing I had then,
besides you and the baby,
was my polka dot dress,
I loved your motorbike,
who couldn't like what
that thing did for you.
I remember you selling it,
how your heart poured sadness,
until you hit the accelerator
in the beaten up Cortina and it took off".
When you said. "It's OK,
I'm a father now".

Then she said,
"I promised myself back then,
as soon as I earn enough
I am buying you ten motorbikes"
and "Baby,
I still wear that polka dot dress".

Peter Lavery

Tea Dance

He does the soft shoe shuffle
across the carpet
marks a slow glissade
around the doorpost
transfers his weight
before his hesitation-waltz
to the sink, fills the kettle
pauses in his pirouette
to reach tea bags, pour the milk.
As he trips the light fantastic
over the lino's edge I reel
him safely in, lead a close conga
back to the table where settling
we find ourselves all of a tango.
Have you ever seen an old-fox trot?
Tally-ho!

Caroline Vero

The Harbour Bar, Toronto

You'd ordered beer when I got there
although you knew I drank wine.
You told me your last five years' history
then asked for mine.

But my heart clenches and cringes
when I return to this city:
I couldn't express how I'd loved you –
the grief, the pity

of the lost years I'd cherished your absence
while my life didn't bear fruit;
of how we'd failed one another.
I sat there, mute

with no words to say I was sorry,
that both of us were to blame.
The city lights danced in the water
with tails of flame.

Anne Ballard

Twilight song

Take me
said she
an officer's lady
one grey afternoon
in the retirement home

I'll take you next summer
said he
a small town Reverend
as they watched another day pass

I'll phone the hotel
and book two rooms
said he brightly
no, just one room
she chided
alright then
he countered
one room two beds
No said she softly *one bed*
Oh you <u>are</u> a naughty girl!
He beamed

The consequence was
they did not go
for soon after
aged 88
she died

Once
as in a dream
he raised his head
and launched
their words again
upon the evening air

And his son heard

Barry Jones

Here and Now

Is set on a hill facing east and west.
Its ceilings are high, its windows clear.
The house where we live is called Now.

At the back are the acres of Then,
Whose hinterland eerily blurs into mist.
Its language is Remember; its lively encounters
Dust.

From the front of the house, lamps
In delicate line lead to an equal obscurity.
But each has a name: Next and After
And When; and some have the names
Of days of the week, or of months.
The last light you see is almost invisible.
It is called Finally.

Where we live is Now. The light falls
Specially, moment by moment,
On books, voices, sights, smells.

There is left-over rain on the rose. The blackbird
Waits by the garden door.

R V Bailey

Dad

He was no Chesty Bond with tanned muscles
straining to escape a snowy-white singlet,
and we teased him for his spread-eagle walk –
asked why his horse had left without him.

His sap-black hands could split a log
in seven strokes, leg-rope and bail
a dozen cows then strip their udders dry
and once a year, wring a rooster's neck
to provide our Christmas dinner.

The tying of hair bows, changing of nappies,
tip-toeing into a baby's room were not for him.

Yet one night when the power went down
and we pulled our chairs into the orange glow
from the stove's flickering firebox, he brought out
a violin with three broken strings and stuttered
some yarns of dancing nights, roller skating days

but Mum blushed and shushed him as he began
a story of riding a bike through the night-time bush
that lay between their family farms and we were sent
to bed with no more than a glimpse of the man
we only knew as Dad.

Kaye Lee

Violin

Salvaged from a totter's cart
a symbol of my father's hope
for me, at least,
if not for him.
My child's hands stretched to reach the strings.
From his rag and bone life,
the fervent wish
that I should play
the lead violin.
Now middle aged,
my father dead,
the violin lies in its dusty case,
the music waiting.

Vicky Olliver

for Molly at 100

I will stroke you with feathers infused
with oil of lavender and attar of roses;
I will loosen your years with beeswax
blended to dews of honey, unroll bandages
of withered flesh and crumbling mind
which keep your child-self confined
and dumb. Now we can go together,
a shuffle at first, then a walk, faster
and faster until we are running toward
the western mountain beyond the town
and there I will call to all the birds
of your homeland – rosellas, kookaburras,
galahs – and as the lyre bird performs
his arcane dance, they will lift you up.

Kaye Lee

Snapshot

Sorting through the old snaps I'd brought you
you remembered perfectly the stout woman
squatting beside the breakwater, stockinged legs
flung out on the sand: 'Mrs Permain!' you said
effortlessly reaching back seventy years to when
I was too young to remember. This was
our childhood, you seven years older, and now
I bring you these blurred records you love, our
past, turning them over, holding them close
for scrutiny:'Oh yes, that's Nellie next door.'
Yet you can't recall what I said minutes
ago. Does it matter? You are so happy
in our game of remembrance. 'Bring me
some more,' you say,'next time you come.'
And I will. Oh I will, before that light is snuffed
out.

Maureen Duffy

Last Rites

Eyes strain at the waning of the Cornish sun
over the chequered fields and skewbald ponies,
the grey-white tumble of cliffs and cottages
to the swishing taffeta sea.

I can still hear the morning's burr-soft country greetings,
see the gull with the broken wing, the green tugboat ease
around the harbour's curve, angling the wharf-stones.

Along the creaming edge of a wave skips a child,
firmly rounded as a hazelnut, clutching a slanting kite.
The soft breeze from the Point tosses the last pouting sail

Dorothy Phillips

Via Cola di Rienzo, Rome

All these delectable young men
sailing towards me, faces a sea
of Caravaggio's beguiling boys

hair clinging to their poised heads
self possession retained in air
tangible as oil, bags of shopping
about their knees.

I fancy I might ask one out tonight
to sport his new Gucci
or Calvin Klein for me.

This city makes me ridiculous
and bold, makes me look
for things that are past reclaiming.

It forgets that I am old
in moments such as these
when my heart finds possibility
shimmering momentarily as it passes.

Lyn White

Under London

Sweat and tears
Push and flow
Holding onto other peoples body's

Suits, Jackets, Ties and Trousers
Soaking wet and smelly,
Girls with tattoos all over their bodies

And the men but with faces covered too.
Pins in noses, breasts and other painful places
Black, White, Green and Yellow

Every one is going somewhere
Some unsure of what they'll find.

Brian Ball

The Journey

I stumble across the bridge
Waterloo to the National.

If only I were a bicycle owner,
With great mobility!

I take refuge in my folding seat,
Open my prayer book.

Hannah Kelly

Amsterdam refocussed

Deep from the basketwork
spider's web-weave

bar silhouettes
through distorted glass

jewellery box chimes
ripple heartbeat canals

ghosts from the ghetto catching the camera,
cigarette smoke curling

a shiver of rain
in this city of bicycles

monochrome steel sparking trams
smother the screech to central

arms crossed hard on her breastbone
she holds all her colours in

photographs flatten
grey shapes from the sea.

Juliet Troy

Sign Your Name, Kafka

Sign your name, Kafka.
Sign it on the basement wall
Of Two Celetna St
Where meals are served by candlelight.
And you above those years before
You played alone, but
Did you know that basement, Kafka
Ever run down there to hide
From your father's voice, his rage, his eyes
To find the place you found inside?

Sign your name, Kafka
Sign it in the basement
Of Two Celetna St
Where now they serve expensive wine
That patrons sip by candlelight
And did you touch the dimness, Kafka
Of that basement then
Feel the coolness of the stone
Did you sign your name there, "FRANZ"
When you were missing and alone?

The Kafka family lived in a flat in 2 Celetna St in Prague when Franz Kafka was five years old.

Tim Harris

Bergkamen Power Station

A band of ten in white hard hats
are walking over metal grids,
are marvelling at great steel pipes,
are gazing into hellish depths
beneath their feet. Resounding noise
drowns out all talk. The warmth is strong
and close.

Our bearded engineer
has shown us on his diagrams
the furnace and the turbine room,
explained how crates and furniture
get cleaned and shredded for the plant.

Through a round glass I peer and see
an orange whirl of flames and sparks:
beneath the skin of the machine
the fiery present builds itself,
now through the steel I feel it surge
and all its tethered serpents rise.

Dennis Tomlinson

Who's Looking?

Diggers and drills knock old Beijing up
into nostrils and lungs and the blackened barks of trees.
Picture him here in this haze that blocks the sun
among the Gucci bags and Starbucks, and the only rickshaw
a straining metal monument.

Dust from his China may be in my head, but his China
is not mine nor mine his, for this is a country
where sleepy rivers have been smartened up and ordered off
to service rice-fields and factories. Come down,
come down into the stink of this hutong,

come down to the bicycling grandmothers, and look –
a sweet-potato-seller! Breathe the earthy steam,
get the scald of the flesh. Come and sit on a k'ang,
split melon seeds with your front teeth. Spit.
Belly-laugh again.

He will lift up his eyes beyond the concrete and steel
towards the little hills around Hailung –
not all of them have been carted off for cities.

He will look to where the Thousand Peaks
still point the way like spires.

Frances Thompson

Votive Offering

To be young. In a take away dwelling.
Night and day. Rhodes old town.
A kid of a Greek. Slicing flakes
of lamb off a skewered carcass.
Watery eyes narrowed to a margin of meat.
Another souvlaki pushed as tight as a cry,
into its paper cone, housed by fragments of salad.
Some chips as well says a voice.
Perturbed, he throws away the late afternoon
dead chips. Cuts open a freezer bag and drops
fresh carbohydrate into a pan
of sizzling oil, coating everything.
Will you holiday at the end of the season?
Amazed, he half looks at the voice's face,
snaps out, maybe two days rest,
then Spain and another job like this.
His back faces customer. Chips frenziedly salted.
No. No. Just vinegar. He drops them, insanely hot,
drowned in malt, into their fragile waiting cone.
They burn the hand, of the body, of the voice,
of the face he keeps lowering his eyes too.
Just a kid. Always working in high season.

Alan Price

At Blake's Lock

I had forgotten the river,
its sound and its waterfall,
the green of it;

forgotten the launching
of birds, the heron's
plastic watchfulness,

its only movement an eye,
a feather-flick; forgotten the reach
of trees, their branch-dipping

offerings and tang
of pillow-soft leaves;
forgotten the sun's marbling,

its mirror-darts of quiet,
secret dreams; forgotten
the scoop of oars,

glide and scull of boats;
how we closed our eyes,
white-blinded by the sky,

but could still see; how time
rested on a blade edge,
unblemished, cloud-light.

At Blake's Lock I remembered
these weir-real things,
and the rush of them, and you.

Claire Dyer

Birling Gap to Bristol in an Old Red Citroen with the Sun-Roof Open

The child is clean, dressed for sleep,
clutches a tub of cucumber cubes

is carried to the car at dusk -
the day too hot to leave before.

The mother straps him in his fortress
massages her aching back

he prattles on, then all is quiet -
the mother sighs away the day.

Miles to drive in the cooling night
the luxury of silent air.

Past Seaford, stars begin to show
first bright ones, then a heavenful.

She looks behind and is amazed,
he's awake, watching, calm.

The child asks –
How d'you know where to go?

She says – *See that star,*
it's shining over Bishopston.

The child watches hour by hour,
the star sees them home.

She goes to lift him from his seat;
he says – *I want to walk.*

Chrissie Williams

They'll Never Tame Billy Caspar

After Judd killed Kes, I went barmy.
Ah could a killed Judd, but he'd joined 't Army.
Ah were right mithered,and wished ah were dead,
but summat kept whisperin' in me 'ead.
"They'll never tame me".That's worrit said.
So, ah went down 't fuckin pit instead.
Couldn't abide it. Worst place in't world.
Onny lasted a week, then a hurled
me snap tin down't shaft and laffed
all the way 'ome. They said ah were daft.
But they'll never tame me.
Then ah joined 't Army, an that were worse.
Marchin and runnin' (and learning to curse)
But ah decked our Sergeant, and, well that were that.
from Army to dole queue in seven weeks flat.
But they'll never tame me.
So I started out nickin. Did that for a bit.
Then o'course I got nicked. Eeh, I were such a tit.
So I did me time and inside ah read books.
They thought ah were mental, the gormless fucks.
I let em walk through me:couldn't give a shit.
Like that day when I laughed and walked out o't pit.
But they'll never tame me.

Ah read all ah could about falcons an all.
Ah read and ah read till I climbed up the wall.
Ah knew it all. Left nowt to chance.
No time for't pub or Friday night dance.
Then ah went to the park, where the falconer worked,
and persuaded 'im to let me 'elp. He jerked
me around at first, but then he could see
ah knew more than he did, and gradually
I took over. Then finally, he quit.
And the falconer? Well, it's me. I'm it.
And they have tamed me.

David Osgerby

Black Dog

Liking a ball is one thing,
but demanding I like it too, that was inspired.
He lay there chewing the ball,
saying this is good. The steady chomp
of his jaws said *I love this thing*
and he leant hard against me
biting as rough as he could.
Looking at the tennis ball I said
"You're saying that this ball is mine aren't you,"
His eyes smiled back, confirming
I spoke "Good dog" and suddenly
I sure did want to steal that ball.
I offered him the only thing I had, an empty bottle
and he walked off in contempt..
He threw the ball high into the air
planning on catching it again,
but somehow his trick backfired
and the ball flew easily to my hand.
His teeth banged into the backs of my fingers
as he tried to snatch it back.
It hurt but did no harm,
I felt the punishment fit the crime
and hoped for further leniency
if I gave the ball straight back,
I did - knowing I could steal it again.
Any time.

Peter Lavery

two black dogs

running after balls
their owners wearing red and green
picking up pebbles to skim the water
one sail boat defines the sea
a little girl in pink on a pink bike falls
her daddy straightens it

a little white dog
scottish with his tail jumping
walks his owner carrying a poo bag

some more tricycles come
the girl in pink keeps falling
rides onto the lawn in front of which
the bike path runs   then the pebble beach
dark backed gulls

my friend the watercolourist
dips her brush blurring the horizon
paints the red green and pink
two charcoal spots
for the black dogs returning
mouthing their balls

Juli Jana

Tomato

The ripe tomato had taken patience and daily care to grow
It had known the sprinkling of the water can, the tomato food
                              brought to and fro
It had known three others on the stem, heavy ones not light
One beneath, two above, to the left and to the right

It fell a little early maybe
Prised 'twixt thumb and finger
Plucked from the tree
Succulent fruit it lay on earthenware dish to be plunged
                              through by a very
                              sharp knife
Into eighths, quarters or simply slices
It was one of my pleasures not vices

I wrapped it up with care
It was the first item of my fare
I snapped it up in a few minutes of my break

Maybe next year there'll be more
Maybe next year there'll be four

Ann Barefoot